Everyone Feels
SCARED
Sometimes

by Marcie Aboff   illustrated by Damian Ward

PICTURE WINDOW BOOKS
a capstone imprint

Thanks to our adviser for his expertise:

Terry Flaherty, Ph.D., Professor of English
Minnesota State University, Mankato

Editor: Shelly Lyons and Jennifer Besel
Designer: Lori Bye
Art Director: Nathan Gassman
Production Specialist: Jane Klenk
The illustrations in this book were created digitally.

Picture Window Books
151 Good Counsel Drive
P.O. Box 669
Mankato, MN 56002-0669
877-845-8392
www.picturewindowbooks.com

Printed in the United States of America in North Mankato, Minnesota.
092009
005618CGS10

All books published by Picture Window Books
are manufactured with paper containing at
least 10 percent post-consumer waste.

Library of Congress Cataloging-in-Publication Data
Aboff, Marcie.
Everyone feels scared sometimes / by Marcie Aboff ; illustrated by Damian Ward.
p. cm. – (Everyone has feelings)
Includes index.
ISBN 978-1-4048-5756-8 (library binding)
ISBN 978-1-4048-6115-2 (paperback)
1. Fear–Juvenile literature. 2. Fear in children–Juvenile literature. I. Ward, Damian, 1977-
II. Title.
BF723.F4A36 2010
152.4'6–dc22   2009024063

Everyone has feelings. Sometimes people feel happy. Other times people feel sad. People can feel angry or scared, too. These feelings are normal.

HAPPY

SAD

ANGRY

SCARED

There are many ways to show how scared you are. There are many ways to feel less afraid, too.

Josh hears loud thunder.
It sounds like the world is splitting apart!
Josh feels his heart pounding fast.

Josh runs to find his mom.

His mom tells him he is safe.

Deanna gives a book report.

She squeezes her hands into fists
as she talks.

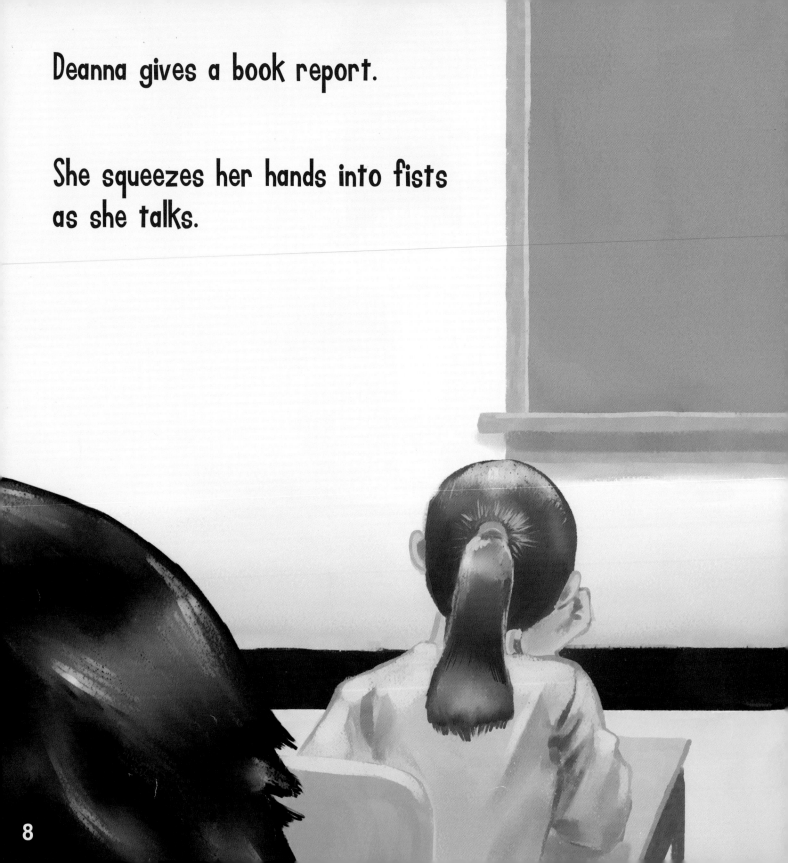

Deanna takes a deep breath.
Her hands relax.

Derek sees Mrs. Johnson's dog. Derek hides behind his dad.

Mrs. Johnson holds the dog's leash tight. She tells Derek that her dog likes his back patted. Derek softly pets the dog's back.

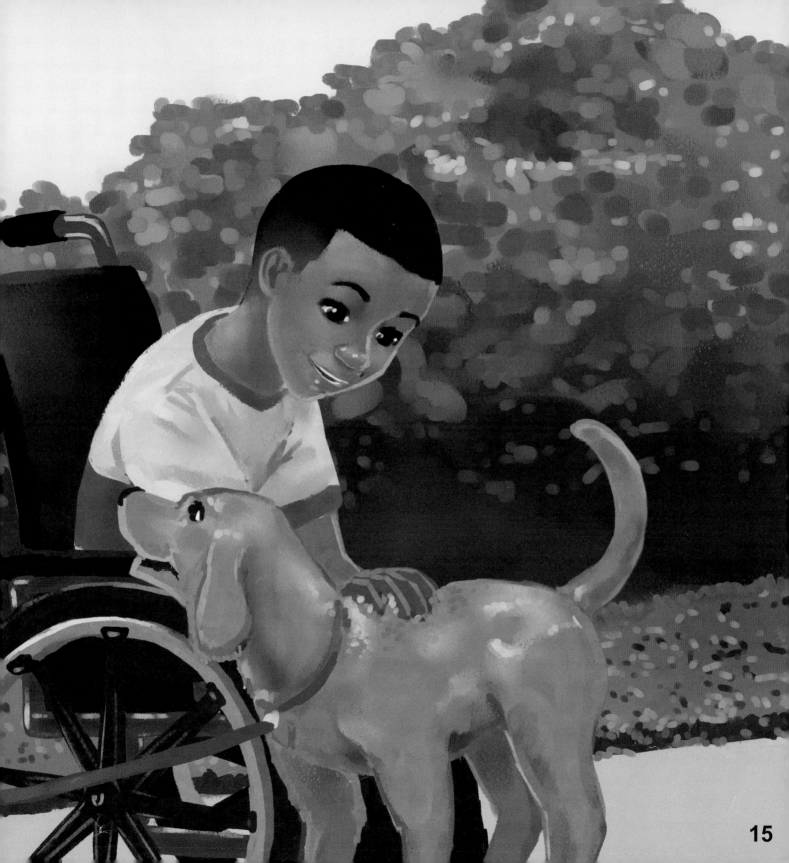

Katie's room is dark. She thinks about scary monsters. Katie starts to shake.

16

Katie turns on the light. She cuddles with her favorite blanket. Her mom tells her that monsters aren't real.

Leo is riding the Ferris wheel
for the first time. He rises
high in the air.

Leo screams.
It's a long way down!

Leo holds on to his older brother's hand.
Leo closes his eyes.

He thinks about being on the ground again.

Things to do when you feel scared:
- Talk to an adult about your feelings.
- Take deep breaths until you feel calm.
- Cuddle with your favorite blanket or stuffed animal.
- Take small steps to get over your fear.
- Think about something that's not as scary.

Glossary
feelings—emotions; anger, sadness, and happiness are all kinds of feelings.
relax—to become free from a tight or excited state
scared—filled with fear

More Books to Read
Annunziata, Jane, and Marc Nemiroff. *Sometimes I'm Scared.* Washington, D.C.: Magination Press, 2009.

Moroney, Tracey. *When I'm Feeling Scared.* Columbus, Ohio: Gingham Dog Press, 2006.

Wilson, Karma. *Bear Feels Scared.* New York: Margaret K. McElderry Books, 2008.

Internet Sites
FactHound offers a safe, fun way to find Internet sites related to this book.
All of the sites on FactHound have been researched by our staff.
Here's all you do:
Visit *www.facthound.com*
FactHound will fetch the best sites for you!

Look for all of the books in the Everyone Has Feelings series:

Everyone Feels Angry Sometimes

Everyone Feels Sad Sometimes

Everyone Feels Happy Sometimes

Everyone Feels Scared Sometimes